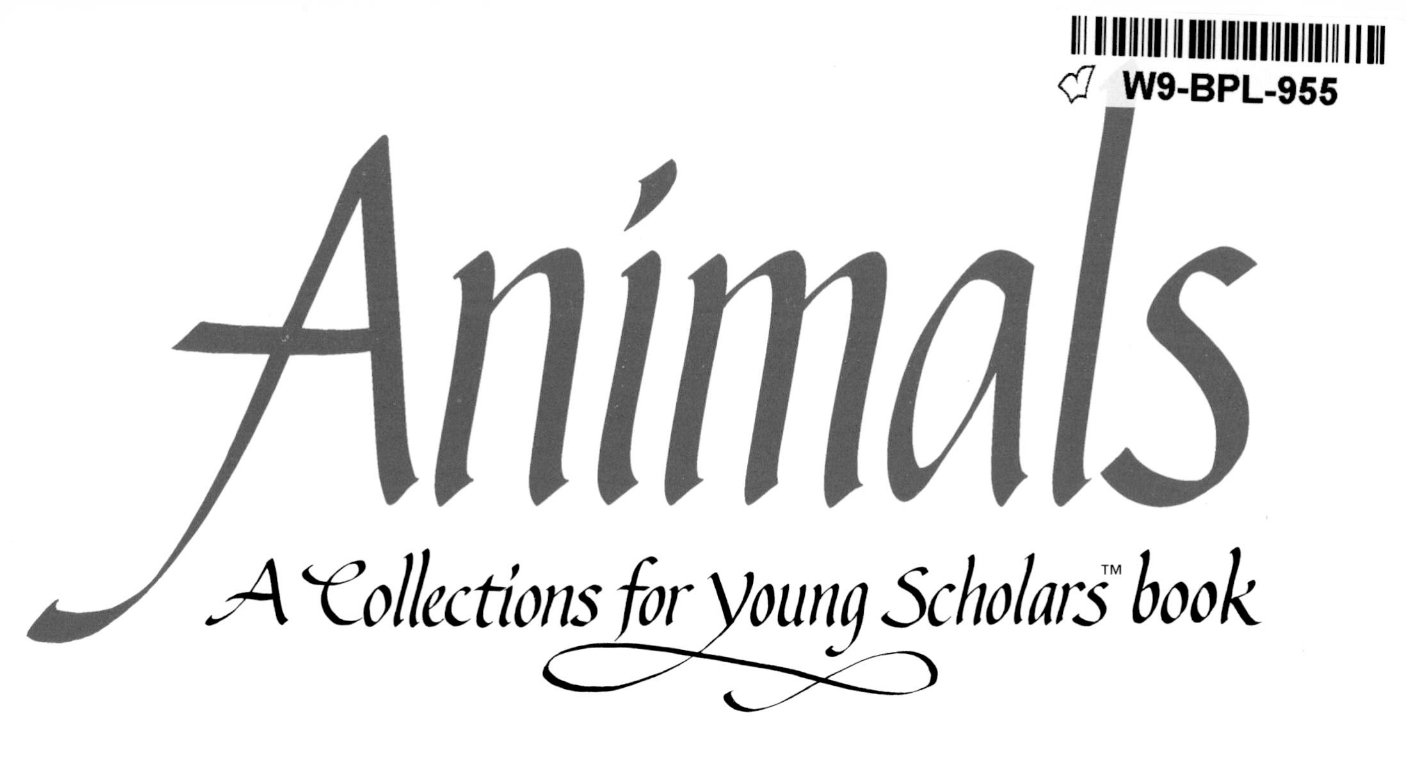

OPEN COURT PUBLISHING COMPANY
CHICAGO AND PERU, ILLINOIS

PROGRAM AUTHORS
Marilyn Jager Adams
Carl Bereiter
Jan Hirshberg
Valerie Anderson
S. A. Bernier

CONSULTING AUTHORS
Michael Pressley
Iva Carruthers
Bill Pinkney

CHAIRMAN
M. Blouke Carus

PRESIDENT
André W. Carus

EDUCATION DIRECTOR
Carl Bereiter

CONCEPT
Barbara Conteh

EXECUTIVE EDITORS
Nancy Dyer
Shirley Graudin

SENIOR PROJECT EDITOR
Nancy Johnson

ART DIRECTOR
John Grandits

VICE-PRESIDENT, PRODUCTION AND MANUFACTURING
Chris Vancalbergh

PERMISSIONS COORDINATOR
Diane Sikora

COVER ARTIST
Normand Chartier

Printed in the United States of America

ISBN 0-8126-0247-1

10 9 8 7 6 5 4 3 2

ACKNOWLEDGMENTS (PHOTOGRAPHY)

14 © Erwin and Peggy Bauer/Bruce Coleman Inc.
© L. & D. Klein/Photo Researchers, Inc.
15 © Joe McDonald/Bruce Coleman, Inc.
© Jeff Foott/Bruce Coleman, Inc.
© Karl Ammann/Bruce Coleman, Inc.
16 © Arnold Crane/Tony Stone Worldwide
© Hans Reinhard/Bruce Coleman, Inc.
© Jane Burton/Bruce Coleman, Inc.
17 © Johan Elzenga/Tony Stone Worldwide
© Tom McHugh/Photo Researchers, Inc.
18 © Stephen Dalton/Photo Researchers, Inc.
© Karl Ammann/Bruce Coleman, Inc.
19 © Erwin and Peggy Bauer/Bruce Coleman, Inc.
© Darryl Torckler/Tony Stone Worldwide
© Robert Noonan/Photo Researchers, Inc.
20 © John Shaw/Bruce Coleman, Inc.
21 © Halle Flygare/Bruce Coleman, Inc.
© Joseph Van Wormer/Bruce Coleman, Inc.
© Patricia Robles Gil/Bruce Coleman, Inc.
22 © John Visser/Bruce Coleman, Inc.
© Rod Planck/Tony Stone Worldwide
© Joe McDonald/Bruce Coleman, Inc.
23 © J. Barry O'Rourke/The Stock Market
© Tom Tracy/The Stock Market
© Pedro Coll/The Stock Market
© Karen Leeds/The Stock Market
© Bryan F. Peterson/The Stock Market
© Christel Rosenfeld/The Stock Market

CONTENTS

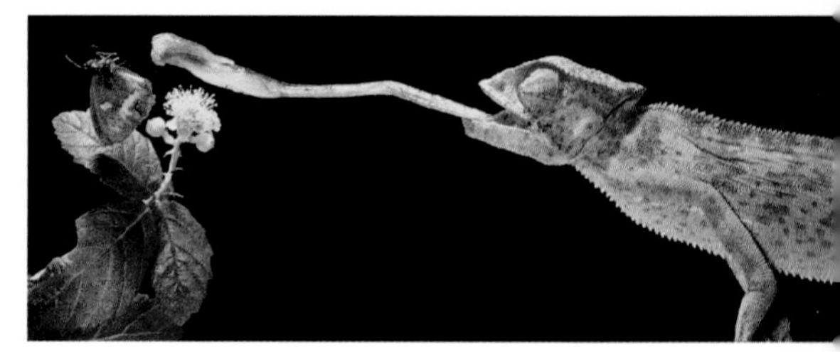

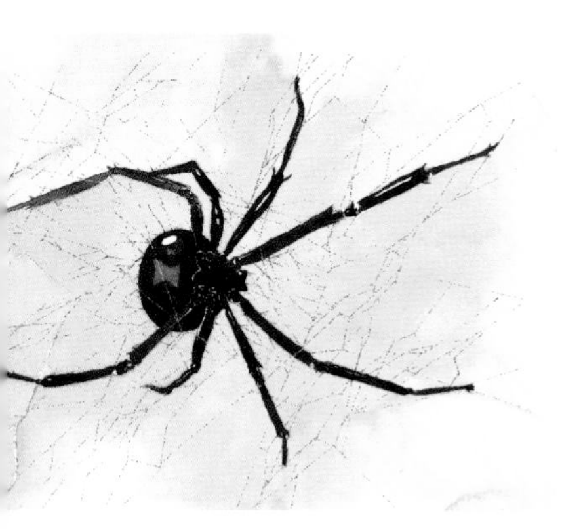

RACCOONS

Jacki Fishman Santoro

illustrated by Irene Brady

See the raccoon babies!
They are called cubs.

Mother raccoon finds
food for her cubs. They like
to eat fish and corn and nuts.

Soon the cubs will be
two months old.
Then they can find
their own food.

BABY ANIMALS

Carol K. McAdam

illustrated by Pat Traub

Some baby animals look like their parents.

The baby hippopotamus
looks like its mother.
It likes to rest on her back.

The baby zebra looks like its mother.
It likes to run next to her.

Some baby animals
do not look like their parents.

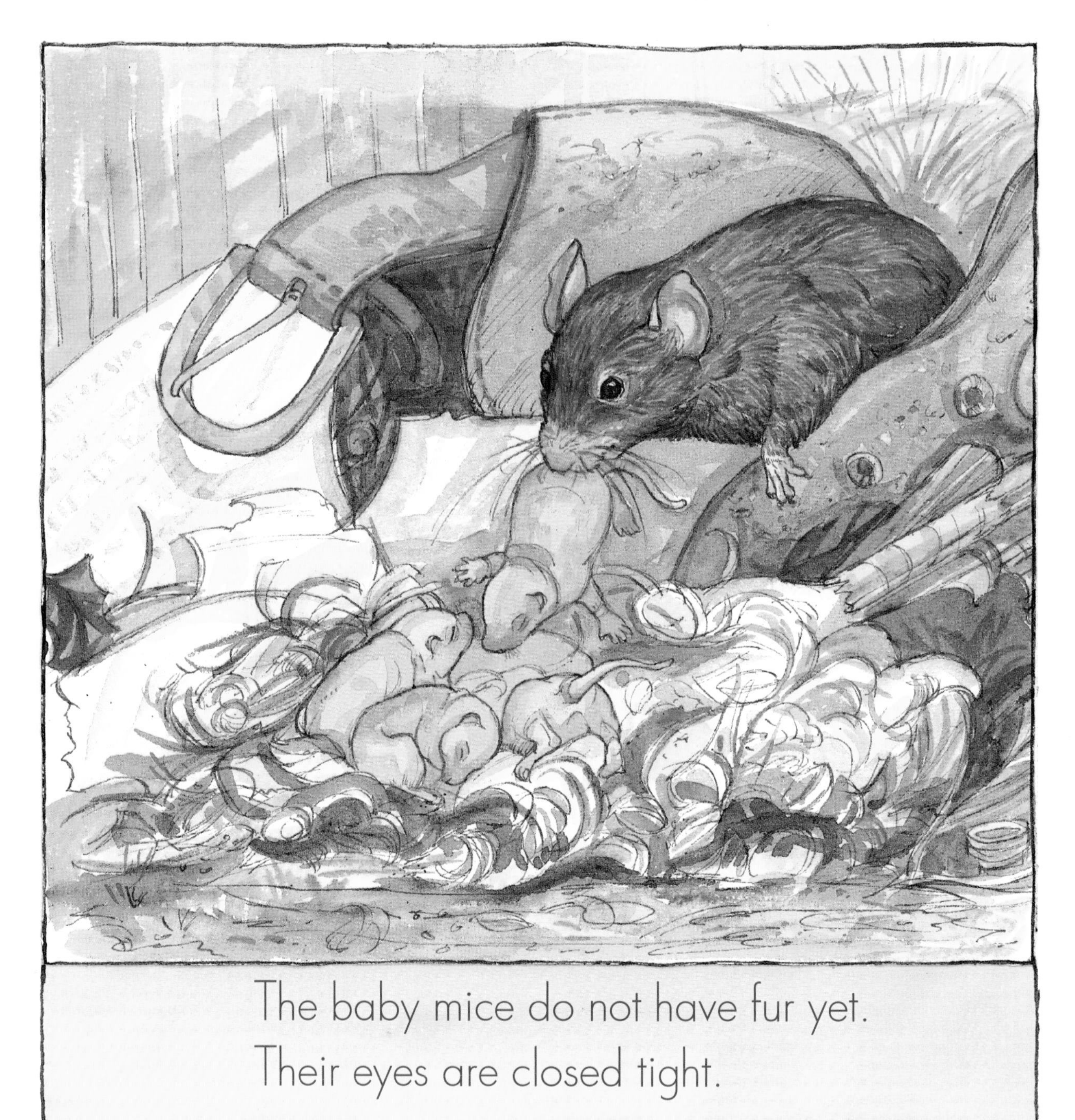

The baby mice do not have fur yet.
Their eyes are closed tight.

Baby animals will look like
their parents when they grow up.

Some baby animals
can take care of themselves
as soon as they are born.

A baby turtle
hatches alone in the sand.
It can swim and find food
without any help.

New baby alligators can
catch food by themselves.

Some baby animals
cannot take care of themselves.

New baby robins do not
have feathers, and they cannot fly.
Father robin brings food.
Mother robin keeps the babies
warm with her feathers.

A baby kangaroo is only
the size of a lima bean when it is born.
Mother kangaroo keeps her baby
safe and warm in her pouch.

When baby animals grow up,
they will have animal babies of their own.

MUNCH CRUNCH:
THE FOODS ANIMALS EAT
by Deborah Eaton

Deer eat grass, flowers, and leaves.

A katydid is a snack for a squirrel monkey.

Munch, munch, munch.
Some animals munch grass.
Crunch, crunch, crunch.
Some animals crunch bugs.

Animals eat many different foods.

Eagles catch fish with their sharp claws.

A toad gulps down a worm.

Gorillas eat banana trees, but not bananas.

A giraffe's long neck and tongue help it reach leaves to eat.

A goat reaches for his dinner.

Some rhinos dig up small trees with their horns.

Some animals eat only plants.

A hungry elephant will try to eat all the leaves on a tree.

Giant pandas eat for ten hours a day.

Plant eaters have to eat a lot of food every day.

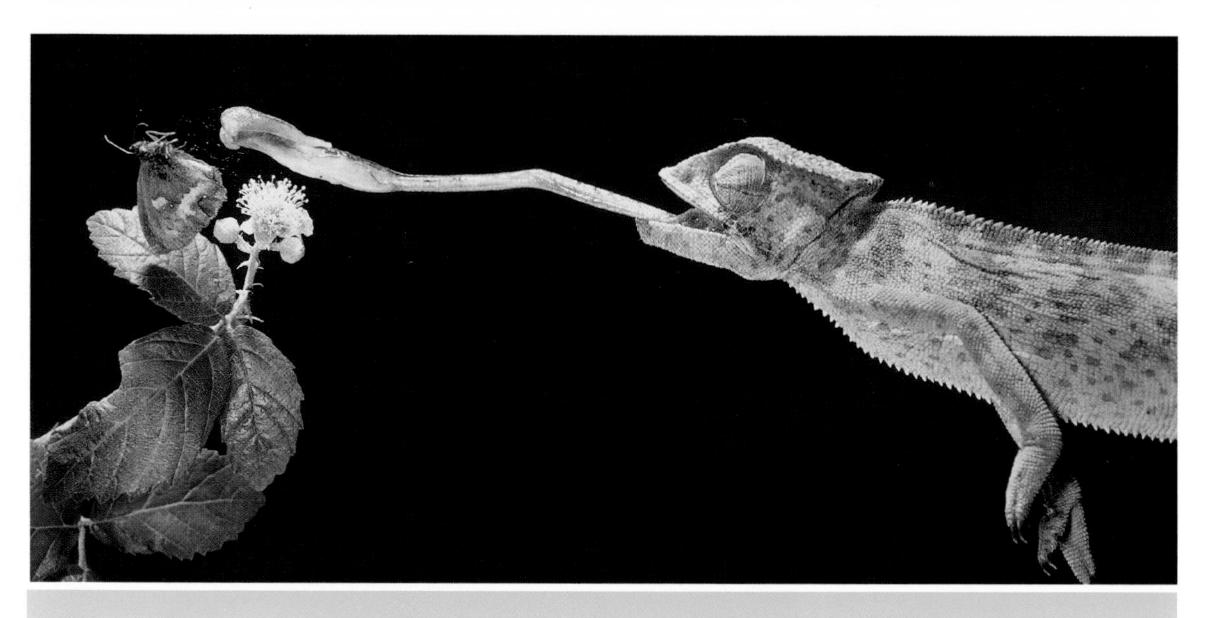

A sticky tongue helps a chameleon catch food.

Lions eat one big meal every three or four days.

Some animals are hunters.
They catch other animals to eat.

Coyotes gobble up rabbits, mice, squirrels, and goats.

Big fish eat smaller fish.

This spider traps food in a web.

A brown bear fishes for its dinner.

Sometimes getting food isn't easy.

Bighorn sheep need grass to eat, even in winter.

Koalas need leaves from one special kind of tree.

Two storks want the same fish. One will go hungry.

A snake's jaws open wide for an egg.

Mice like to eat berries.

This puffin eats lots of fish.

Sometimes animals like to eat the same foods children do.

Deer eat apples.

Chimps eat bananas.

Bears eat honey and nuts.

Sea gulls eat fish.

Raccoons eat corn.

Robins eat berries.

SPIDERS

Carol K. McAdam

illustrated by Pamela Carroll

A fly buzzes in the garden.
It flies from leaf to leaf.

Then it gets trapped in a spider web!

A spider rushes across the web.
It wraps up the fly in silk threads.
Later the spider will eat the fly.

Spiders are hunters.
They hunt for insects to eat.
Many insects eat plants
that people need.
Spiders help people
by eating the insects.

Many spiders make webs to trap insects.

A web is made of silk. The silk comes from tiny tubes at the end of the spider's body.

Even a baby spider can make silk.
The spider climbs to the top of a weed.
Its body makes a little piece of silk.

The wind catches the silk
and carries the baby spider away.
Soon it will make its own web.

THE HERMIT CRAB

Jo Olson

illustrated by Robin Brickman

The hermit crab is an odd animal—even for a crab.

Most crabs grow their own hard shells to keep them safe from other animals.

The hermit crab has no shell. Only its claws and the front part of its body are hard.

The back part of its body is soft. A fish, a seal, or a bird can easily eat the crab.

How does a hermit crab stay safe? It finds an empty shell and cleans it out with a claw. Then the crab backs into the shell.

The crab turns its body until it fits just right. Then it carries its new house wherever it goes.

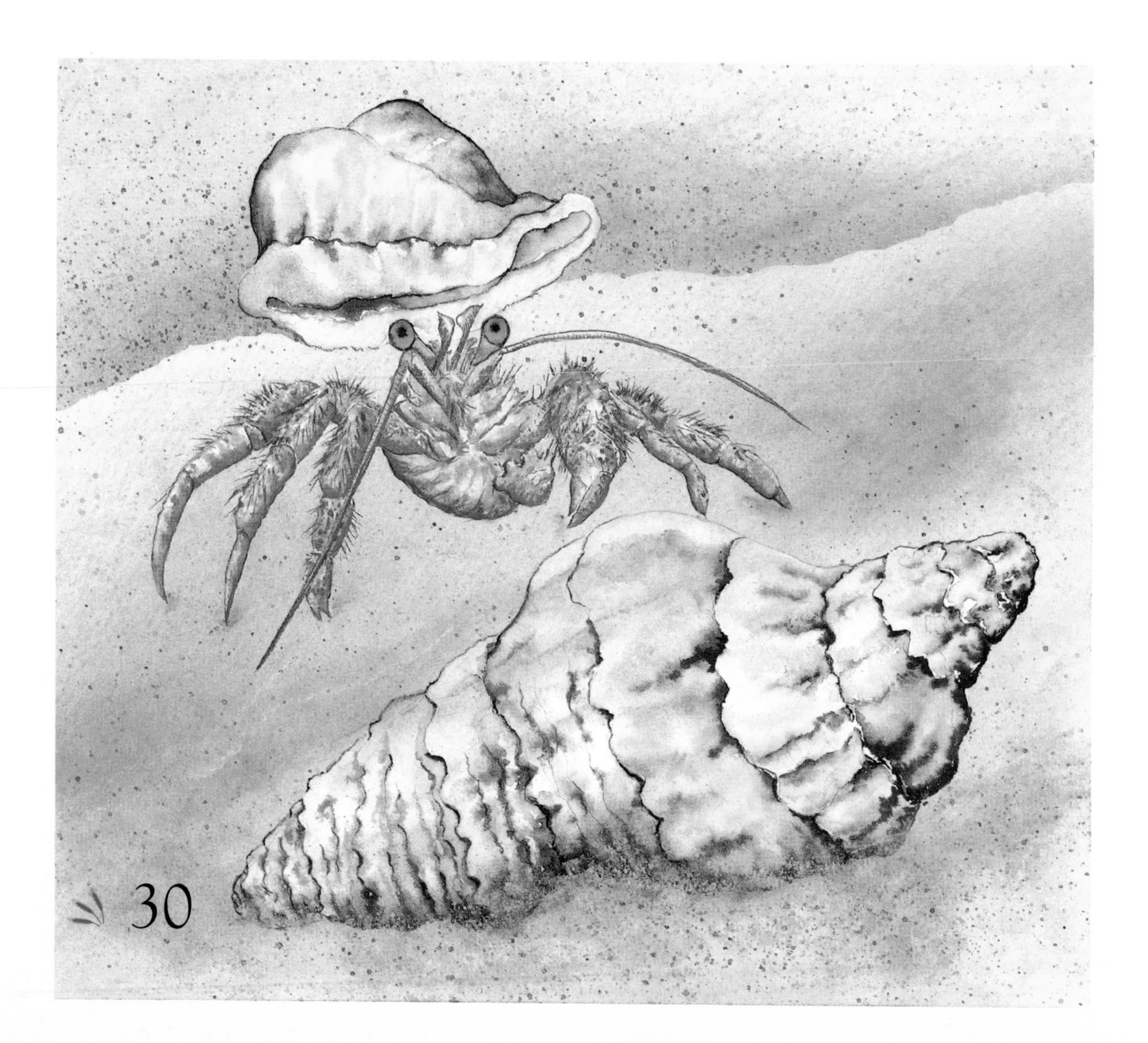

As it grows,
the crab must find bigger and bigger shells
to live in.

If it can't find a shell,
it might move into an empty jar.
It might even steal another crab's shell.

FINE ART
ANIMALS

Detail from a hand scroll showing a cat and a mouse. 19th century. Kawanabe Kyosai.

Ink and wash on paper. The Fletcher Fund, 1937, The Metropolitan Museum of Art. 37.119.1.
Photo: © 1982 The Metropolitan Museum of Art

Tunic. 15th–16th centuries. Coastal Inca, Ica Valley, Pe

Wool and cotton. The Michael C. Rockefeller Memorial Collection, Bequest of Nelson A. Rockefeller, 1979, The Metropolitan Museum of Art. 1979.206.1131. Photo: © 1981 The Metropolitan Museum of Art

Line of Maasai cattle. Collected in Kenya in the early 1960s. Artist unknown.

Paint on tin sheet. Photo: © Peter Beard